INDIGENOUS AMERICAN CULTURES

Celebrating the NAVAJO

ANNE ACCARDI

Mitchell Lane
PUBLISHERS

Parent and Caregiver Tips for Creating Nonfiction Readers

The high-interest topics in the ***Indigenous American Cultures*** series are sure to get your young reader excited about reading nonfiction. While exploring a fascinating subject, your reader will be introduced to new facts, ideas, and vocabulary.

Tips for Reading Nonfiction

Talk about Nonfiction

Explain that nonfiction books provide facts about real-world topics. When readers read nonfiction, they gain a rich understanding of the world. They build background knowledge that provides a foundation for learning and academic success.

Look at the Parts

This book contains the following helpful features. Share the purpose of each feature with your reader.

Photos, Captions, and Graphic Aids
The photos, captions, maps, diagrams, time lines, and other graphic aids in nonfiction texts contain a wealth of information. Help your reader identify different ways information can be displayed.

Sidebars
These extra tidbits of information help satisfy readers' curiosity and expand their knowledge.

Table of Contents
Located at the front of the book, this list shows the big ideas within the text and the page numbers where they can be found.

Glossary
Located at the back of the book, the glossary defines key words and phrases that are related to the topic. These words and phrases can be found in the text in colored type.

Comprehension Questions (Fact Check)
Multiple-choice questions help readers self-check to make sure they understand what they read.

Index
Located at the back of the book, the index is an alphabetical list of topics and the page numbers where they can be found.

With a little help and guidance, your reader will be on their way to enjoying and learning from nonfiction books.

Mitchell Lane
PUBLISHERS

mitchelllanepub.com

2001 SW 31st Avenue
Hallandale, FL 33009

First Edition, 2026.
Author: Anne Accardi
Designer: Rhea Magaro
Editor: Kim Thompson

Series: Indigenous American Cultures
Title: Celebrating the Navajo / by Anne Accardi

Hallandale, FL : Mitchell Lane Publishers, [2026]

Library bound ISBN: 979-8-89260-555-7
Paperback ISBN: 979-8-89260-591-5
eBook ISBN: 979-8-89260-558-8

PHOTO CREDITS
Alamy: Lebrecht Music, 4; Maurice Savage, 5; FLHC FBD44, 7; Witold Skrypczak, 10; John Elk III, 11; ZUMA Press Inc, 15; Alpha Historica, 16, 17; robertharding, 19; North Wind Picture Archives, 21; Hemis, 22, 23; Native American - Indian culture, 23; Danita Delimont, 23; US Air Force Photo, 24; Px Images, 27; Visions of America, LLC, 28; Dreamstime: Carrieemoran, 9; Public Domain: Library of Congress, 6, 8, 18; Wiki/ Keith Allison, 26; Shutterstock: vivooo, cover, 1; RuslanKphoto, cover, 1; George Burba, cover, 1; Reid Dalland, cover, 1; Roschetzky Photography, 5; Alexey_Rezvykh, 8; Elena_Suvorova, 12; Cavan-Images, 13; irisphoto1, 13; Underawesternsky, 14; inacio pires, 20; olepeshkina, 23; Vicki L. Miller, 25; Grindstone Media Group, 27; meunierd, 29, Sabrina Bracher, 29;

CONTENTS

A NAVAJO CONNECTION

Have you ever seen a beautifully woven blanket or rug like the one shown here? If you have, then you already know something about the Navajo. Their traditional "storm" weaving pattern has four corners. The number four is important to the Navajo. Four **sacred** mountains rise above their desert homeland to the north, south, east, and west.

Culture Close-Up

The Navajo homeland is in a region of the U.S. known as the Four Corners because it contains parts of four states: Colorado, Utah, Arizona, and New Mexico.

NAVAJO HISTORY

Hundreds of years ago, the Navajo built a strong society on land that is now the southwestern United States. They hunted, farmed, and gathered wild foods. Beginning in the 1500s, Spanish and American **settlers** moved in. They wanted land from the Navajo and other **Indigenous** tribes. The Navajo fought back.

In 1863, the U.S. Army forced the Navajo to leave their homeland. They were made to walk hundreds of miles to a prison in a distant part of New Mexico. Many people died. The terrible journey came to be called the Long Walk.

At the end of the Long Walk, soldiers kept guard over Navajo people at Fort Sumner, New Mexico.

Culture Close-Up

Once, the Navajo were hunter-gatherers. Then, the Pueblo tribe taught them how to farm. The Spanish taught them to raise sheep.

In 1868, the Navajo signed a **treaty** with the U.S. It allowed them to return to a small part of their homeland. The Navajo Nation reservation was created.

In 1868, many Navajo people returned to their family homes.

Culture Close-Up

In the 1920s, oil was found on the reservation. The tribe let companies drill for oil on some of their land. This earned money for the Navajo Nation and helped it grow into a larger community.

On the Navajo Nation flag, the current Nation is shown in orange. The reservation created in 1868 is brown. Each of the four sacred mountains has its own color. An oil rig is shown along with buildings, plants, and animals that are important in Navajo culture.

EXPLORING NAVAJO PLACES

To learn about the Navajo, you can visit Window Rock Tribal Park. You can see a memorial to Navajo soldiers. You can view the beautiful wind-eroded arch of red sandstone for which the nearby town was named.

Culture Close-Up

In Window Rock, you can also visit the free Navajo Zoo and Botanical Park. On display are plant and animal species that are important to the Navajo culture.

At Monument Valley Navajo Tribal Park, you can drive or hike to see desert canyons, mountains, and **plateaus**. Navajo people have lived in harmony with this environment for centuries. They believe that people should live in balance with the land and with animals.

At Monument Valley, you can spend the night in a traditional Navajo home called a **hogan**. This domed, eight-sided building has one room. It is made from juniper trees and desert soil. A fire pit or stove stands in the center. Your visit will include traditional Navajo stories, music, and dancing.

Culture Close-Up

Hogans are used for Navajo religious ceremonies. They face east so the morning sun can shine in and bring good blessings. The dirt floor and skylight connect to Mother Earth and Father Sky.

THE NAVAJO LANGUAGE

The Navajo call themselves *Diné*, which means "the people." Their language is called Diné Bizaad, and approximately 175,000 people speak it today. It is a **tonal** language that is difficult to learn. Words with different pitches have different meanings.

In the Navajo Nation, the language is used every day. When the Navajo Nation Council meets, its members speak in Diné Bizaad.

Dr. Buu Nygren is President of the Navajo Nation. He often speaks in Diné Bizaad.

Culture Close-Up

Practice these Navajo words and phrases.

Yá'át'ééh (Hello.)

Haash yinilyé? (What is your name?)

aoo' (yes)

dooda (no)

Diné Bizaad bíhoosh'aah. (I am learning Navajo.)

Diné Bizaad has a special place in U.S. history. During World War II, the U.S. military needed a secret code for keeping plans safe. Navajo men were chosen to create and use a code based on their language. They were called Navajo Code Talkers.

The code was used to send more than 800 important messages during the war. U.S. enemies were never able to break it.

Culture Close-Up

The Navajo Code Talkers helped U.S. Marines win the Battle of Iwo Jima.

HONORING NAVAJO TRADITIONS

For hundreds of years, Navajo people have been raising sheep, harvesting wool, and spinning and weaving yarn. The Navajo are known for making beautiful rugs and blankets in bold patterns. The practice is often passed from mother to daughter.

Today, Navajo artists continue the tradition. They use looms to weave yarn spun from local wool. They use handmade tools and natural dyes.

Culture Close-Up

The Navajo raise Navajo-Churro sheep. The breed is highly prized for its wool and meat. The Navajo call these sheep *T'áá Dibé*, or "first sheep."

Growing corn is an important part of Navajo culture. Corn pollen is used in religious ceremonies. On a traditional Navajo farm, corn was planted on the land between canyon walls.

Today, the Pollen Trail Dancers honor their ancestors. They perform dances that carry on Navajo traditions and teach others. Their dances celebrate corn, weaving, and other important parts of Navajo culture.

Culture Close-Up

Corn pollen is yellow powder found on the tassels of corn plants. For the Navajo, it represents life, health, and the sun. It is collected and dusted on people during ceremonies to provide a blessing.

NAVAJO CELEBRATIONS

The Navajo Nation Fair is held each September. It is one of the largest Indigenous American celebrations in the country. Thousands of people come to watch the parade that goes through the town of Window Rock, Arizona.

There are carnival rides, rodeo events, a barbecue, and arts and crafts booths. People eat fry bread and other traditional foods. At the **powwow**, dancers compete for prizes.

Culture Close-Up

Fry bread is deep-fried bread made with flour, lard, sugar, and salt. You can put sweet toppings on it or add meat to make Navajo tacos.

Singing and dancing are important in Navajo culture. Traditional songs are prayers to the Holy People, or gods, who care for the people. Healing ceremonies include bonfires and feasts. Blessingway ceremonies bring good fortune. A singer or medicine man leads songs, prayers, and stories.

At festivals and ceremonies, Navajo people enjoy traditional dances and games. Hoops are used during dances to tell stories and make shapes and symbols.

FAMOUS FACES

Major League Baseball All-Star Jacoby Ellsbury is a member of the Navajo Nation. He helped the Boston Red Sox win the World Series in 2007 and 2013. In 2011, he started a baseball camp for Native American youth.

Nicco Montaño is an American mixed martial artist. She grew up on the Navajo Nation reservation. In 2017, she became the first Indigenous American to win a UFC (Ultimate Fighting Championship) title. She said, "My people are my motivation."

Culture Close-Up

Navajo Corey Witherill is a successful race car driver. He is one of the only Indigenous Americans to ever race in the Indy 500.

LESSONS FROM THE NAVAJO

The Navajo believe that people should care for nature, help others, and think about future generations. They celebrate their past and honor their **heritage**. Learning about Navajo traditions can help all Americans learn to respect each other and work together to make the world a better place.

MONUMENT VALLEY
NAVAJO TRIBAL PAR

GLOSSARY

heritage (HER-i-tij): traditions and beliefs that people consider to be an important part of their history

hogan (HOH-gun): a traditional, domed Navajo house that is built from wood and mud and that has eight sides and a door facing east

Indigenous (in-DI-juh-nuhs): the earliest known inhabitants of a place

plateaus (pla-TOHZ): areas of level ground that are higher than the surrounding area

powwow (POU-wou): a gathering of Indigenous Americans that is organized for social or ceremonial reasons and that may include traditional singing, dancing, and drumming

reservation (rez-ur-VAY-shuhn): an area of land set aside by the government for ownership by an Indigenous American tribe

sacred (SAY-krid): holy, very important, and deserving of great respect

settlers (SET-luhrz): people who make their homes in a new place and who have historically invaded and oppressed Indigenous peoples who originally lived there

tonal (TOE-nuhl): related to how high or low a sound is

treaty (TREE-tee): an agreement between two or more nations

FACT CHECK

1. What place in Arizona is the capital of the Navajo Nation?
   A. Table Rock   B. Phoenix   C. Window Rock

2. What direction does the door of a hogan face?
   A. east   B. west   C. south

3. What war did the Navajo Code Talkers help win for the United States?
   A. World War I   B. World War II   C. the American Revolution

4. What does Diné mean?
   A. the people   B. Navajo   C. language

Answers: 1. C, 2. A, 3. B, 4. A

FURTHER READING

Buckley, James. *Who Were the Navajo Code Talkers?* Penguin Workshop, 2021.

Widener, Leslie Stall. *Kindred Spirits: Shilombish Ittibachvffa.* Charlesbridge, 2024.

Young, Brian. *Healers of the Water Monster*. Heartdrum, 2022.

ON THE INTERNET

Discover Navajo
discovernavajo.com
Explore this tourist site for information about tribal history, culture, and places to explore.

Native American Hall of Fame
nativehalloffame.org
Find biographies of well-known Native Americans from the 1860s to the present.

Navajo Nation
www.navajo-nsn.gov
The official site of the Navajo Nation has information about the tribe's history and culture.

INDEX

ABOUT THE AUTHOR

Anne Accardi is an author from Kansas City, Missouri. She is thrilled to share facts about Indigenous Americans with young people. She loves history and finding ways to connect the past with the present and future. When she's not reading or writing, you can find Anne in a library, museum, or movie theater.